JOSIP LONČAR / HOW TO BELIEVE?

JESMAR PRESS

33-1933

JOSIP LONČAR / HOW TO BELIEVE?

Publisher: Jesmar Press

Translator: Janet Ann Tuškan

Editor: Liggett McLaws

Cover Design: Terry O'Neill

ISBN 953-7065-00-6

CIP – Katalogizacija u publikaciji

Nacionalna i sveučilišna knjižnica – Zagreb

UDK 248.143

LONČAR, Josip

First published in Croatian 2013

This English edition 2015

Introduction

We often find ourselves faced with the unsolvable challenges of unanswered prayer, for which we often do not have an adequate response, so we are almost condemned to say, "It's God's will" or "It's a mystery which we have not been given the grace to understand".

It is certain that life in all its complexity includes the aspect of "mystery" which will only be revealed to us when we leave our bodies and come before the Lord; it is also certain that some crosses in our lives are the means by which God teaches us.

3

My intention is, that after reading these pages, anyone who is honestly seeking God will be moved, with God's help, to analyse some of the "spiritual battles" they have lost, and be encouraged again to pray for the needy.

With this book, I want to help you, my readers, receive what God yearns to give you by faith. Additionally, I want to help you understand the Gospel better, so that you may live it more successfully, and with joy*.

The book has two parts. The first is supposed to help the reader receive, by faith, what God longs to give him. The second is to encourage and teach the reader how to witness to others himself.

I have shared the Gospel in many different countries, in more than two hundred and fifty parishes, and have had opportunities to testify my faith to multitudes of people. I have come to the conclusion that Christianity is without meaning, if we are not constantly changing into better people. This happens through constant prayer, constant learning and constant evangelization.

This book is my contribution to the Year of Faith, 2013, and to the Church's calling for New Evangelization.

Josip Loncar

I. HOW TO RECEIVE BY FAITH

A Parable about Faith

Perhaps you have heard this story: in the middle of a town square, a man strung a tight rope from the church tower to the next building. A crowd of people, just coming out of Sunday Mass, gathered to see what was going on. The man picked up a pole and walked across the tight rope from the church to the other building. The spectators clapped enthusiastically at his skill and courage. The man then shouted in a loud voice: "Do you believe that I can cross over without the pole?"

They replied with one voice, that they believed he could. He did just that. After that, he brought up a wheelbarrow and asked if they believed he could cross while pushing the wheelbarrow. Again the people cried out that they believed. Then, to the great delight of the crowd, he crossed back and forth a few times, pushing the wheelbarrow in front of him.

In this way, he earned their trust. Then there came another question: "Do you believe that I can do the same thing with someone sitting in the wheelbarrow?" Almost all of them replied that they believed, waiting in anticipation.

But his next question shocked them: "Which one of you will climb up here and sit in the wheelbarrow?" Suddenly, the crowd went quiet. No one was willing to climb up and sit in the wheelbarrow!

I wonder if any of these spectators had been brave enough to "sit in the wheelbarrow" during the Mass they just attended. By this I mean, did anyone become spiritually involved or were they just spectators, watching someone (in this case the priest) carry out the sacramental rites?

We can choose to be either spectators at the Mass, or decide to become actual spiritual participants. In a like manner, Jesus can remain on the sidelines of our lives as an observer or, only at our request, become an active participant in all that happens to us.

Jesus' Question

The Bible tells us that many people came to Jesus asking for healings for "various kinds of diseases" (Luke 4:40). Scripture states that "He healed all who were sick" (Matthew 8:16). Yet, He still asked some of them: "Do you believe that I <u>can</u> do this?"

He never asked anyone: "Do you believe that I <u>want</u> to do this?"

Today, we get hung up on that second question, ignoring the first and more important question. What does that second question actually mean? After all, Jesus knew He was capable of doing what they asked of Him.

Many people came to Jesus to be healed by Him or to receive other acts of mercy. He healed all those who came to Him, but still He asked some of them: "Do you believe that I can do this?"

By this time, multitudes of people had seen numerous miracles which were being reported all over Palestine. Thus, the answer to the first question was very easy: "Yes, I believe You can do this; You have proved it many times."

Today we do not even ask this first question. We believe that Jesus is the Almighty God who can do whatever He wants - <u>if He really wants to!</u>

This is where we get hung up on that second question **which Jesus never asked**!

What does this second question actually mean? Jesus knew He could do what they were asking of Him. After all, His miracles were being talked about all over Palestine, so the answer should have been very easy.

If someone answered yes to Jesus' question "Do you believe that I can do this?", His next comment would be: "May it be as you have believed". This question, "Do you believe...?" both then and now, means precisely this: "Is there any way in which you <u>can receive</u> (are able to accept) what I want to give to you?"

Remember that Jesus didn't say "...because you have believed...", but "as you have believed..."*

The phrase "any way in which" refers to our individual ability to accept God's grace: His infinite love, mercy, favor, and goodwill toward mankind. He is asking if the doors of our hearts are open to receive what God longs to give us.

Unfortunately, few Christians are able to answer Jesus' question with a resounding "Yes".

It is not a case of a hard-hearted God who needs to be bribed into giving us what we ask for, but of our willingness to open our hearts to be able to receive it. Prayer does not change God's heart, it changes man's heart. God's heart is overflowing with love; it is not necessary to coerce or coax Him into bestowing mercy on man.

Man is the one who is incapable, due to ignorance, hardness of heart or just plain stubbornness, to receive what God yearns to give him. Man can even reject what God has already given him.

How to Believe?

God knows man's psyche, and He knows that man is limited or only provisionally able, to receive what He wants to give him. When we begin to understand man's role in the exchange of love with God, we will be able to receive much more. This won't happen because God wants to give us more, but because we will be able to receive more.

If we look at Jesus in the Gospels, in several situations we will see how He studied people before He talked to them. It is as though He wanted to find the best possible way to grant them God's mercy/grace. In some situations He took the initiative and determined the way in which He would act, while in other circumstances, He simply accepted the suggestions offered to Him.

In the Gospels, we read numerous testimonies of Jesus' supernatural (miraculous) work. The Gospels talk about healing, deliverance, repentance, miracles, etc. In many cases, it was essentially the basic human need for health, freedom, forgiveness, comfort, truth, which attracted people to Jesus. After Jesus met their needs, in a miraculous way, some of those people wanted to enter into a closer relationship with God.

Our quest for health is still one of the most basic human needs. Contemporary medicine and health care are far from solving our problems so that, even today, Jesus has no reason to change the way He acts toward sick people and anyone else in need.

Throughout the Gospels, we can easily see how much Jesus really cared about finding the most appropriate means to help people in their individual circumstances. He wanted as many people as possible to receive what He desired to give them.

Jesus is the same today*. He is still seeking the most appropriate means to be allowed to heal each of us. Yet, we rarely realize that His healing relies upon our personal ability to be open to receive from Him.

Take a look at the Gospels and see what Jesus is showing us. Study Him at the moment when people were asking Him for something - the way in which he responded to their pleas. He sometimes simply allowed them to determine the way He acted, but not always. Look at these two typical examples.

Envision each line as a separate scene of the event. We should not move to the next line before creating a mental picture of the preceeding one. Like Mary, keep these things (remember everything) in your heart and ponder upon them (Luke 2:19).

In this first example, Jesus allowed people to determine his actions:

When they had crossed over,

they came to land at Genezaret

and moored the boat.

When they got out of the boat, people at once recognized him,

and rushed about that whole region

and began to bring the sick on mats to wherever they heard he was.

And wherever he went, into villages or cities or farms, they laid the sick in the market-places,

and begged him

that they might touch

even the fringe of his cloak

and all

who touched it

were healed. (Mark 6:53-56)

This second example presents a different manner of healing:

They came to Bethsaida.

Some people brought a blind man to him

and begged him to touch him.

He took the blind man by the hand

and led him out of the village;

and when he had put saliva on his eyes

and laid his hands on him,

he asked him, 'Can you see anything?'

And the man looked up

and said, 'I can see people,

but they look like trees, walking.'

Then Jesus laid his hands on his eyes again;

and he looked intently

and his sight was restored,

and he saw everything clearly. (Mark 8:22-25)use kjv

(underlined by the author)

In the first case, Jesus accepted the suggestions of the people and did exactly what they expected Him to do. In the second He, alone, determined how He would heal the blind man.

Luke 5:17 reports that the power of the Lord was present with Jesus to heal. In the next chapter, he begins his report on the Sermon on the Mount, by writing that this power healed and delivered all those present. Luke was a physican which gave him a different perspective as far as healings were concerned. He made this statement:

And all in the crowd

were trying

to touch him,

for power

came out from him

and healed all of them

(Luke 6:19)

Now we should ask ourselves some interesting questions:

Why did Jesus not act the same way everywhere He went, since this method had proved to be so incredibly successful and simple?

Why wasn't it enough for these people to touch Him to be healed, as in other locations?

Why did He sometimes ask people if they believed?

Was His power any less in other places?

Were the sick people elsewhere sick to a greater or lesser degree?

Was His will different in different places?

What is God's Word trying to tell us here?

In the second example, we can see that Jesus did not accept the suggestion made to Him. Why not?

Why did He need to take the blind man outside the village and then, in addition to laying hands on him, also put saliva on his eyes? Was Jesus' faith, power, will, or something else, insufficient at that moment, so that He had to use another method?

If we recall how He healed the sick by simply speaking a word*, we have to ask ourselves what was different in situations similar to this one in which he <u>needed to</u> spit in the blind man's eyes!

Look at a few typical examples of Jesus' methods when He was healing or delivering people:

As the sun was setting,

all those who had any who were sick

with various kinds of diseases

brought them to him;

and he laid his hands

on each of them

and cured them. (Luke 4:40)

That evening

they brought to him many who were possessed by demons;

and he cast out the spirits -

with a word,

and cured all

who were sick. *(Matthew 8:16)*

And once again:

When he had said this,

he spat on the ground and made mud with the saliva

and spread the mud on the man's eyes,

saying to him,

'Go, wash in the pool of Siloam'.

Then he went

and washed

and came back able to see.

(John 9:6-7)

(underlined by the author)

What does the Word say to us?

What does Jesus want to teach us?

Do we recognize in these descriptions different methods that we can use when we pray for the healing of the sick?

Does this mean that Jesus could have healed everyone in the same way, but He used different methods to teach us something?

Today, in Catholic parishes, the most frequent prayers for healing occur through the sacrament of the anointing of the sick. This sacrament contains several different biblical methods of prayer for healing, that is, several different ways Jesus used to heal people. It includes speaking the Word, laying on of hands, anointing with oil, and the possibility for the sick to touch Jesus' Body in the consecrated Host. (He is actually physically present in the consecrated Host as long as the bread lasts in our body.) Still, this sacrament is not used as effectively as it could, and should be.

Let us return to the Gospels and consider a few facts.

As Jesus returned from being tempted in the wilderness, the power of the Holy Spirit was upon Him, and in that power He continiued working for the next three years, without a break.

Jesus was not well understood in His home town of Nazareth and, as a consequence, "He could there do no mighty work"; only a few people were able to receive healing (Mark 6:5). A similar situation exists in Jesus' Church today because many people still don't understand Him.

From all this, it seems that the way Jesus acted depended more on those He was serving, rather than on Himself. And that is the key - Jesus knew that some people could only receive God's grace in certain prescribed ways.

The situation has not changed today. Assume that you, as you read this, are sick or have some other problem you would like God to resolve. How could this happen? How do you expect this to happen and why in that particular way?

If, in our individualized opinion of how God should act, there is at least one way we can receive from Him, that means we have a distinct hope or expectation. In that case, we can anticipate with a degree of confidence. The surer we are that our method will work, the greater our confidence will be. What does our personal conviction of receiving God's grace depend upon?

Let's try to explain this with a commonly-held belief.

We Catholics know that the intercession of saints is available to help us in certain situations; that is, different saints are able to intercede for very specific things. There is a widespread belief that St. Anthony of Padua can help us find lost things. Millions of people around the world can attest that, through His intercession, they miraculously found something that was lost.

During his life time, however, St. Anthony was noted for many more miracles than just locating lost objects. Then why is it that most people employ his services only for "hide and seek" situations? Why do we trust certain saints only in narrowly defined circumstances? Has God made it that way because of what the saints did during their lives, or have we come to that conclusion on our own?

Jesus is the God-man who performed miracles in a variety of ways. Still, many people trusted Him only if He acted in the one way they expected. In some places, they wanted to touch

Him, in others they wanted Him to lay hands on them and, in still other places, they expected another behavior altogether.

Jesus, literally, could have healed each sick person in any way He chose. But the act of healing did not depend solely on what Jesus could do, but also on the way in which these people were able to receive his miracles.

Let us return to the saints. Hypothetically, can all the saints intercede for any type of grace? Of course they can! Why then do we not have confidence in them?

Why, for example, do so few of us pray to St. Peter to intercede for healing? Because we, personaly, have never heard of his doing that. We know that he healed many people during his life time, yet we are not able to accept this possibility for our own lives.

Most of us do not trust that St. Peter is capable of interceding for healing. If someone we know testified that he had prayed to St. Peter, and told us the exact way he had prayed, then we could accept the possibility. After that, we could believe that St. Peter actually can intercede successfully for healing, and we could follow that very same method of prayer. Just think about that!

Let Me Touch You

Now, consider Jesus' method of teaching, in the following example from the Gospels. Focus your attention on every single word, not only to view the scene, but also to experience it, frame by frame:

Now when Jesus returned,

the crowd

welcomed him,

for they were all waiting for him.

Just then there came a man

named Jairus,

a leader of the synagogue.

He fell at Jesus' feet

and begged him

to come to his house,

for he had an only daughter,

about twelve years old,

who was dying.

As he went,

the crowds

pressed in on him.

Now there was a woman

who had been suffering from haemorrhages

for twelve years;

and though she had spent all she had

on physicians,

no one could cure her.

She came up behind him

and touched the fringe of his clothes,

and immediately

her haemorrhage stopped.

Then Jesus asked,

'Who touched me?'

When all denied it,

Peter said,

'Master,

the crowds surround you

and press in on you.'

But Jesus said, 'Someone touched me;

for I noticed

that power

had gone out from me.'

When the woman saw that she could not remain hidden,

she came trembling;

and falling down before him,

she declared

in the presence of all the people

why she had touched him,

and how

she had been

immediately healed.

He said to her,

'Daughter,

your faith

has made you well;

go in peace.' (Luke 8:40-48)

I find this to be one of the most interesting, and most beautiful, stories in the Gospels. All three synoptic writers describe it in detail. What actually happened?

Jesus was surrounded here by a large crowd. He was on His way to Jairus' house. Jairus' only daughter was there, dying. Every minute was important. The people, in their desire to see what would happen, "surrounded" and "pressed" in around Jesus. A woman, who had been hemorrhaging for twelve years, approached Jesus from behind, touched the fringe of His robe, and was immediately healed.

In that pressing and pushing crowd, Jesus stopped and wanted to know who had touched Him. That question seemed ridiculous as Jesus was being jostled on all sides. Jesus persisted, but people denied touching Him.

Peter could not understand what was happening. He only knew that Jesus needed to hurry to Jairus' house. After all, Jairus was the head of the synagogue and a very important man. All of us should learn a vital lesson here: all people were, and are, equally important to Jesus!

The woman, realizing she had been discovered, explained what she had done and the reasoning behind her actions. Why didn't she simply ask Jesus to lay hands on her or use some more conventional method? Why did she decide to touch Him from behind? What was going on in her mind and her heart? Anyone, who had been waiting to be healed for twelve years, would certainly have looked for a doctor, first of all. That is what she had done, time after time, until her money ran out.

Finally, she heard that a great prophet, Jesus, was doing things no Old Testament prophet had ever done. Undoubtedly, she already knew about one of the most famous "healing" prophets, Elisha, and was comparing him to Jesus. Elisha had a formidable reputation*, so her fear of Jesus was completely understandable. She probably recalled a passage in the Old Testament's Second Book of Kings, and built her confidence (faith*) upon it:

So Elisha died,

and they buried him.

Now bands of Moabites

used to invade the land

in the spring of the year.

As a man

was being buried,

a marauding band was seen

and the man was thrown

into the grave of Elisha;

as soon as the man touched the bones of Elisha,

he came to life

and stood on his feet. (2Kings 13:20-21)

God's anointing (the presence of God's power) was on Elisha's bones. It was so powerful that it could bring a man back from death itself. We can relate, as we remember how much the Church has revered the relics of great saints, down through the ages.

This woman's belief made Jesus so happy that He praised her in front of everyone, calling her "daughter" and acknowledging her faith. He clearly said that she was healed because of her faith, not because of His will. *('Daughter, your faith has made you well.)*

Many people witnessed this event, but the Gospel writers don't tell us if others present followed her lead.

We know that on many other occasions people followed her example*. Turning our attention to Jesus' famous sermon in the region of Gennesaret, thousands there only wanted to touch Him and, everyone who did, received healing. Why were they healed, while the people who witnessed the woman's healing were not? When you witness something extraordinary and understand it, you need time to meditate on it for your heart to receive it. Why does this not happen to us when we touch Him in the Eucharist?

Perhaps the witnesses to this woman's healing did not have enough time to meditate and receive faith in their hearts. One reason why they did not succeed could have been their curiosity to discover how the situation with Jairus' daughter would turn out!

Assume that the hemorrhaging woman lived near Gennesaret, and that many people there knew her plight. When she appeared, glowing with health and testifying about her miracle, it is reasonable to assume that local people began to envision themselves healed in the very same way. They had enough time to meditate, and then open their hearts, to be able to receive.

Think back to the blind man whom Jesus healed by spitting in his eyes*. If we realize that various healings had taken place in the same region where he lived, including the healing of a deaf and dumb man (Mark 7:31-35), this blind man's healing becomes easier to understand. This is another instance when Jesus used the unexpected method of healing with His saliva. Many people would have heard about that healing, and our blind man probably did as well.

Local people also might have known the case of the blind man whom Jesus healed by making mud from his saliva (John 9:1-8). What would you expect if you were blind? Wouldn't you be thinking that Jesus' saliva could give you sight? Wouldn't you be imagining that scene and expecting the same result? Jesus could read the blind man's mind and knew that his heart was open to receive healing in one way only, by using His saliva.

In a totally unrelated miracle, Jesus surprised everyone by saying "Your sins are forgiven!" In this case, Jesus healed a paralytic man, after forgiving his sins (Matthew 9:1-8; Mark 2:1-11; Luke 5:18-25). If we study these three reports carefully, we will see that, apart from Jesus' clear declartion of His authority to forgive sins, this passage implies something else extremely important.

Look at Mark's account:

When he returned to Capernaum after some days,

it was reported that he was at home.

So many gathered around

that there was no longer room for them,

not even in front of the door;

and he was speaking the word to them.

Then some people came,

bringing to him a paralysed man,

carried by four of them.

And when they could not bring him to Jesus

because of the crowd,

they removed the roof above him;

and after having dug through it,

they let down the mat on which the paralytic lay.

When Jesus saw their faith,

he said to the paralytic,

'Son, your sins are forgiven.'

Now some of the scribes were sitting there,

questioning in their hearts,

'Why does this fellow speak in this way?

It is blasphemy!

Who can forgive sins but God alone?'

At once Jesus perceived in his spirit

that they were discussing these questions among themselves;

and he said to them,

'Why do you raise such questions in your hearts?

Which is easier, to say to the paralytic, "Your sins are forgiven", or to say, "Stand up and take your mat and walk"?

But so that you may know that the Son of Man has authority

on earth

to forgive sins'

34

he said to the paralytic—

'I say to you,

stand up,

take your mat and go to your home.' (Mark 2:1-11)

The Gospel writers suggest to us that Jesus saw the faith of the men who brought the paralytic. If we consider the implications, we will realize what probably happened: it was the faith of the paralytic's friends, not his own, that Jesus worked with. He recognized the paralytic's understandable discouragement and disbelief. The paralytic probably considered himself a sinner, thinking God would never listen to him in his sinful state.

Down through the centuries how many believers have had this very same attitude in their hearts? How many have failed to receive God's mercy as a result of this misapprehension?

Are there other instances in the Gospels, where Jesus forgives somebody's sins before He heals him? **Not a single one!**

If we study the Gospel further, we find many passages where Jesus healed <u>every single person</u> in the crowd, without exception. Were they all without sin - all humble, all good, all merciful? Of course not!

Was this privilege reserved only for those living at the same time as Jesus - to come to Him and be healed, regardless of their sins? Of course not!

Why, then, do most people think they need to be sinless before they can receive God's grace? Actually, God's grace is intended especially for sinners, to heal them and set them free!

Jesus loved the paralytic and healed him in the only possible way the man could receive his healing. He, personally, forgave all the man's sins and thus, removed the fetters that had prevented his belief. Otherwise, why would He forgive his sins? The man certainly did not ask for it.

Everything that Jesus said to the scribes was intended to persuade the paralytic to accept forgivness. Only when that barrier had been removed was the man able to receive his healing. If we have the same problem, we now know how to resolve it!

The Converted Blasphemers

I have frequently witnessed God healing unrepentent sinners, without their ever asking for forgiveness. He truly did love us while we were still sinners*.

In one parish, after Mass, I prayed for the sick. During the prayer, I said that God was healing someone with a permanently injured hand. His doctors had said he would never be able to clench his fist again. After the prayer, people began testifying about their own healings. From the back of the church, a man started pushing his way through the dense crowd, grabbing people with his clenched fist, as he came. Many people knew him, and they were amazed at the way his hand had been restored.

Taking the microphone, he said: "You all know me as someone who curses a lot. No one has ever been able to stop my blaspheming before. I came to church today out of curiosity, to see these 'so-called miracles' which take place when people pray.

"During the prayer, I certanly didn't expect anything, because I always have blasphemed and would never dare to pray. But, when I heard the words describing my case exactly, something happened inside me, and I cried out to God. At that moment, some kind of power came into my hand, but even more into my heart. As you can see, my incurably damaged hand is healed but, more importantly, my heart also has been healed. If anyone ever hears me blasphem again, then he can shoot me dead!"

On another occasion, I was traveling in Austria with a man, Slavko, who swore so much that I had to get out of the car several times to give my soul a rest. I began to pray quietly for him, and the Holy Spirit inspired me what to do. I asked about his wife, and he told me, sadly, that she had a bad heart and needed open heart surgery.

I told him that God still heals the sick and invited him to a parish where we regularly prayed for the sick after Mass. He decided to bring his wife the next Sunday. We prayed for her and then, I asked if he wanted prayer for himself. He refused, so I explained this prayer could also help his wife, and he agreed. Of course, we prayed for him to be filled with God's love so he could stop blaspheming.

A week later, they received his wife's medical results, showing that she no longer needed an operation. I asked if anything had happened to him, as well. He said no, but he had noticed something strange. His colleagues at work and, even the neighborhood children, had started to curse, for absolutely no reason. This really bothered him!

His wife then revealed that they had not just begun cursing, but that it was he who had stopped blaspheming, immediately after our prayer. He could no longer tolerate anyone cursing.

It happened that Slavko's father also used to blasphem. This time the deliverance required several years of prayer, fasting and sacrifice on Slavko's part. One day, his father simply stopped blaspheming and persisted until the day he died.

Jesus knows that one of the quickest paths to conversion is the healing/deliverance of sinners.

Open Yourself

Catholics can find many opportunities to receive God's grace: Mass, prayers, shrines, the sites of apparitions, pilgrimages, novenas, vows, etc. In my life, I have seen many examples of these.

We all know about Lourdes, Fatima, Medjugorje, Knock, San Giovanny Rotondo, Guadalupe and many other places where millions of pilgrims have received God's grace: love, mercy, healing, forgivness, conversion and so forth. Grace, of course, is readily available at holy sites because they have been soaked in the prayers of the faithful over the years. Pilgrims go there with hope and confidence, based on what they have heard.

Anointing of the Sick

I have to point out that, in theory, each believer could receive from God whatever He wants to give, but still many receive too little.

Anointing of the sick is a sacrament based on this passage from the Epistle of James:

Are any among you sick?

They should call for the elders of the church

and have them pray over them,

anointing them with oil in the name of the Lord.

The prayer

of faith

will save the sick,

and the Lord will raise them up;

and anyone who has committed sins

will be forgiven. (James 5:14-15)

(Josip - fix below) **This Bible** passage tells us that sick people are so important to God than He wants not just one, but several of the church elders to go to pray for the sick. The serious illness of an individual believer is so important to God that He wants church elders, regardless of their other duties, to go in person to the sick person and pray for him. Later, we will see that the Church, in CCC 1516 also requires this from the elders.

It would be advantageous if priests had plans already in place to alert parishioners when someone is suffering from a terminal illness. Then everyone would know who needs prayer for salvation and/or healing and could spend time praying for their fellow parishioner and his family, at the time of their greatest need.

Personally, if I were seriously ill and in danger of dying I, certainly, would want the entire parish community praying on their knees for my salvation and healing. Blessed is the parish, and the priest, who introduces this practice.

This is what the Church has to say about receiving God's grace through the sacraments:

(CCC 1128) From the moment that a sacrament is celebrated in accordance with the intention of the Church, the power of Christ and his Spirit acts in and through it, independently of the personal holiness of the minister. Nevertheless, the fruits of the sacraments also depend on the disposition of the one who receives them.

(CCC 1516) Only priests (bishops and presbyters) are ministers of the Anointing of the Sick. It is the duty of pastors to instruct the faithful on the benefits of this sacrament. The faithful should encourage the sick to call for a priest to receive this sacrament. The sick should prepare themselves to receive it with good dispositions, assisted by their pastor and the whole ecclesial community, which is invited to surround the sick in a special way through their prayers and fraternal attention.

(underlined by the author)

I know a priest, I will call him Father R., who pays special attention to how he shares the sacrament of anointing of the sick. He says it is his greatest obligation to visit everyone who is seriously ill and to offer them this sacrament. The seriously ill are in danger of dying, and Father R. knows that one day he will have to give an account to God for every parishioner entrusted to his care.

When he visits any sick person, Father R. points out that there is nothing in his parish more worthy of his attention than the healing/salvation of this sick person. Father R. then tells him, in detail, about several remarkable cases of God's grace.

Some people have been healed of serious illnesses, while others have received extraordinary strength and grace to bear their illnesses with peace and love until they died. A number have received the comfort of the Holy Spirit, enabling them to forgive and be reconciled to everyone. Still others have been helped to make a good confession and die in peace.

After that, Father R. explains the sacrament itself: the special power of the holy oil and the way it was blessed, the power of the words spoken and many other details.

The words and rites are explained so they can be clearly understood. These words fall into the sick person's heart like seed, from which God's mercy can grow*. The oil will release the power of the Holy Spirit, which will either heal the sick person or give him supernatural strength to bear his illness.

After anointing the person's forehead and hands, Father R. also anoints the affected area of the body, if possible. He advises the person to let the oil remain, untouched, to sink into his body and act as the most powerful medicine. He reminds the sick person about the power in Elisha' s bones, the woman who touched Jesus' robe with faith and the crowds of people healed by touching Jesus. Father R. invites him to touch Jesus in the Eucharist, expecting His touch to heal him.

The Gospels tell us that the power of the Spirit went out from Jesus and healed people*. That same power, the Church believes, is present in the holy oil used in the sacrament of anointing the sick.

As Father R. lays hands on the sick person, he prays for as long as he thinks necessary for that person to receive grace. After that, Father R. promises to pray until the person is either healed or called home to be with Christ. If he thinks it expedient, Father R. visits the sick person several times, until he is sure that person has been touched by God's mercy in some way.

Nothing is more important than human life, (life on this earth and eternal life in heaven). Any parish, whose priest believes that the eternal life of his parishioners is more important than all else, is truly blessed! If I am ever in need of this sacrament, I would want this priest to visit me.

A priest's primary responsibility is to prepare believers to be able to receive what God wants to give them in the sacraments. However, a great deal depends on a right "disposition" (attitude/openness) in our hearts.

A sick person sees God through the priest. He hears the words of faith and trust in God through the words spoken by the priest. He seeks God's love in the priest's actions. How will he believe, if he does not see faith in the elders of the Church? The example of the elders, in their approach to the sacraments, can have a powerful effect, for good or for evil, on the faith of that sick person, as well as on the entire parish community.

We will all die one day and most of us, as we are leaving this earthly life, would like to know we have the fervent prayer support of our entire parish community. It is up to us to establish this ministry!

II. EVANGELIZATION

The Foundations of Evangelization

A Christian organisation in the USA conducted a survey of 14,400 Christians from various denominations. They queried only those who took their faith seriously, and proceeded to live it. They asked just one question: "What brought you to the point where you began to truly believe in Jesus Christ?" The results were astounding!

I have asked the same question in my native country of Croatia, and the results were almost identical in both countries. 75%-90% replied that it was the personal testimony of a friend or relative which made them think seriously about their faith and, consequently, change their relationship with God.

There are many different opinions about what evangelization is. In this book, I ask you to consider evangelization as sharing faith experiences with others. This may enrich your own picture of evangelization.

The Parable of the Talents

A talent, at Jesus' time, represented a large sum of money, something like two years' salary. Many of you have heard that talents represent the natural, God-given abilities the Lord has given us, enabling us to serve. I suggest that, for the duration of this book, we consider talents as the personal experiences we have had with God. Consider 'trading in talents' as sharing our testimonies about what we have experienced. If our testimonies can persuade just one person to believe, or strengthen his shaken faith, or receive from God what we ourselves have received, then we have traded well.

Let us read, once again, the well-known parable of the talents:

For it is as if a man, going on a journey, summoned his slaves and entrusted his property to them; to one he gave five talents, to another two, to another one, to each according to his ability. Then he went away. The one who had received the five talents went off at once and traded with them, and made five more talents. In the same way, the one who had the two talents made two more talents. But the one who had received the one talent went off and dug a hole in the ground and hid his master's

49

money. After a long time the master of those slaves came and settled accounts with them. Then the one who had received the five talents came forward, bringing five more talents, saying, "Master, you handed over to me five talents; see, I have made five more talents. "His master said to him, "Well done, good and trustworthy slave; you have been trustworthy in a few things, I will put you in charge of many things; enter into the joy of your master." And the one with the two talents also came forward, saying, "Master, you handed over to me two talents; see, I have made two more talents." His master said to him, "Well done, good and trustworthy slave; you have been trustworthy in a few things, I will put you in charge of many things; enter into the joy of your master." Then the one who had received the one talent also came forward, saying, "Master, I knew that you were a harsh man, reaping where you did not sow, and gathering where you did not scatter seed; so I was afraid, and I went and hid your talent in the ground. Here you have what is yours." But his master replied, "You wicked and lazy slave! You knew, did you, that I reap where I did not sow, and gather where I did not scatter? Then you ought to have invested my money with the bankers, and on my return I would have received what was my own with interest. So take the talent from him, and give it to the one with the ten talents. For to all those who have, more will be given, and they will have an abundance; but from those who have nothing, even what they have will be taken away. As for this worthless slave, throw him into the outer darkness, where there will be weeping and gnashing of teeth." (Matthew 25:14-30)

Many people today are true believers, although they have only one talent, one experience. Nevertheless, many people have become priests, missionaries, and even saints, on the basis of only one experience when God revealed Himself to them.

Many Christians have had an experience which is precious to them, but no one has ever encouraged them to reflect upon it and to use it to evangelize. As a result, they are not effective witnesses, as they could be.

If we know how to testify to the right person, at the right time and, in the right way, then we know how to evangelize. If we have had several experiences like this, we will be able to testify to more and more people. Still, even one talent is quite enough to use many times to bring people to God, as we ourselves were brought. Unless we, like the "wicked and lazy slave", bury that one talent!

Truly, if we can testify about one experience, we will be given more talents. Each time we see how God really has changed human hearts through our testimony, we gain a new personal experience, an additional talent. Thankfully, our God is not excessively demanding. If we have five talents, then He asks us to find five others who will receive our testimonies. With His guidance, we should be able to find many more!

Experience as Evangelization

The Apostle Paul, one of the greatest evangelists of all time, wrote:

"When I came to you, brothers and sisters, I did not come proclaiming the mystery of God to you in lofty words of wisdom... My speech and my proclamation were not with plausible words of wisdom, but with a demonstration of the Spirit and of power...(see 1 Corinthians 2:1-5).

Paul knew that successful evangelization demonstrates the Holy Spirit and God's power. He also says that he would not venture to speak of anything except what he had experienced himself (Romans 15:18). He spread the Gospel by taking what he had experienced, reflecting upon it and then sharing that experience with others.

We, ourselves, can have three different kinds of experiences:

1. Experiencing what God has done and is doing in our own lives;

2. Witnessing experiences of God's work in the lives of other people;

3. Listening to and/or reading the testimonies of people whose experiences we have not seen, in person.

There are three different groups of people to whom we need to pass on our experiences of the living God:

1. Atheists or non-Christians

2. Nominal believers who have been baptised, but who do not live out their faith in an active way

3. Christians who actively live out their faith

There is no one who does not need constant evangelization. It encourages us, warns us, lift us up and comforts us. It can come in various forms. Many of us love reading stories about the lives of saints, especially those in which the work of the Spirit and the power of God are described. The most widely read articles in Christian magazines are the testimonies of people who have experienced God in some way. The most interesting homilies during Mass also contain testimonies.

Teaching about God, without testimonies, does not produce the results that it might. This will be clearer when we look at different aspects of evangelization. They are:

1. Jesus Christ as our personal Savior and Redeemer

2. God as the almighty, heavenly, just and loving Father

3. The Holy Spirit as the sanctifier, teacher, guide and constant co-worker in prayer and in life

4. The Kingdom of God consisting of good angels, evil spirits (fallen angels), saints, souls in purgatory, the Father, the Son, the Holy Spirit, and so forth,

5. The Church with its sacraments, liturgy and devotions

Faith is not founded on knowledge about God alone, but also on our personal experience with God. Each of us can receive knowledge about any of the above areas, but we will only live in their full blessing when we have some personal experience of them.

1. Jesus Christ, Savior and Redeemer

Too many Christians today live according to the rules and moral standards of their society, which rarely agree with God's commandments. As a result, they do not feel sinful, not realise their need for salvation. Talk about salvation is far beyond their ability to understand. Only when they find themselves severely tested by life, will some of them begin to think about God and sin. One example of sin is abortion.

Suppose you have a friend at work who recently had an abortion. She might have done it at her husband's insistence, even though she did not want to. Afterwards, she began to fall into depression, experience mood swings and to withdraw into herself. Her conscience was working within her because of what she had done. Not all women who have abortions experience their consciences convicting them, but many do.

So, knowing her problem, you choose a good moment to witness about your own experience of forgiveness (not necessarily for the same sin), or you tell her about another person's experience that has impressed you. You do not need to mention her sin as you do this. She has enough guilt already;

you do not need to add to it. What she does need is light at the end of the tunnel. That light is Jesus Christ.

In such situations, it is enough to use the words: repentance, confession, forgiveness and peace. If you do this, your testimony (talent) can enable the soul of one person to be saved in his or her time of testing. When you see that she has listened to you and received reconcilliation, you can suggest that she join, or return to, the Church while offering to support her on that path. Encourage her to pass on her experience, of Jesus Christ as Savior and Redeemer, to others as well.

After that, allow the Holy Spirit to lead you to the next person whose soul He has prepared for your witness. When you come to the end of your journey on this earth, only God will know how many people have come to salvation as a result of your "trade" in the one talent He entrusted to you.

Shared testimonies produce a desire within other people to have the same experiences. First, they envision what could happen to them, then they yearn and pray. Each of these experiences is as valuable to them as the talents in Jesus' parable.

Here is one such testimony, which you can use:

Finally Free!

A girl told me about her experience with Jesus as Savior and Redeemer from sin. Clearly, she did not have the courage to witness to anyone, that is, to trade in the one talent she had been given. She decided, however, to invest it in a "bank" so the Master would at least receive interest on it. In that way, she was sure to avoid the condemnation received by the man who buried his "one talent". If we can find a good "bank", perhaps our profit will be greater than if we traded ourselves.

I know, for a fact, that the testimony of this girl has been read by thousands of people and I, myself, have told it to thousands at various meetings. Her testimony (talent) will continue to be heard by a great many more people, if God gives me long life. Many, who have already heard or read it, have been touched; and many will continue "to trade" with it in the future.

What that person, in her humility, believed to be quite insignificant, has proved to be a real pearl.* I would like to encourage you, by her example, to do the trading yourself, to pass on your personal testimony about what you have experienced with God, to anyone who will trade with it. Your experience (your talent) can do a great deal of good. It is up to you to be bold and dig it out and invest it in the bank.

Read this girl's testimony and be encouraged to write your own, following her example!

"Like most traditional Catholics, I went to confession twice a year, at Christmas and Easter, because that was what you are supposed to do. I never saw this as anything of much importance or gave it much thought. I went to "get it done". I thought that priests only heard confession twice a year, and that was why there were such long lines outside the confessionals. This always annoyed me.

"However much everything inside me told me that it was a waste of time going there, and that I could give it a pass, some kind of "fear" still drove me to go. I thought that if I didn't go to confession and Christmas or Easter came, while I was still in my 'petty sins', I might end up in Hell.

"When I was little, I loved going to Mass on Sundays, reading the Bible at home and listening to people talking about God. I will never forget the joy I felt when I came out of the confessional for the first time. I was just nine years old. That was the day when I literally skipped all the way home. Since then I never missed a single "compulsory" confession, but the experience of my first confession was never repeated. Sometimes I would wonder why that was, but I didn't make much effort to find the reason.

"For years the sins I confessed were the same, and I would list them off in the same order. I knew that a sin that I was aware of committing must not be overlooked or kept silent, so while I was waiting in line for confession, I tried hard to think about them as little as possible, so I wouldn't have to mention them all. What I didn't know was that I never actually repented. I only learned later that it was not only important to list my sins, but it was equally important whether I felt repentance for the sins I listed, whether I had really made a firm decision not to sin any more, and to be better toward myself, those around me and above all, toward God.

"The years of growing up and maturing passed like lightning. Busy with school, later university, romantic relationships and incidental things, I increasingly neglected anything to do with God. In time, I felt worse and worse, although I had everything I wanted and never lacked anything. I felt so unhappy that several times I literally wished I could leave my body behind. I suffered mood swings, from complete deadness to hyperactivity.

"My dissatisfaction grew and grew from day to day. I felt an overwhelming need to talk to someone. For months, I wondered who I could talk to. Finally I decided to visit a psychologist. 'If nothing else, I will pay someone to listen to me', I thought. I would at least feel a little better after that, but I didn't.

"One evening I went to see a friend with whom I talked for a long time about how I was feeling. She was also going through a very hard time in her life. She had started going to see a psychiatrist but, at the same time, she was talking to a man at church who had helped many people. She told me that he was a man of faith and that, if I wanted to, I could talk to him. Without any hesitation I said I would.

"That conversation lasted four hours, and most of the time I just cried. I was surprised that someone, a complete stranger, would make his time available to me, without any limitations, not asking for anything in return. He told me that I had to make a confession of my whole life, and that if I did, most of my problems would disappear. I thought it was strange that something like confession could solve everything I had been struggling with for such a long time. I decided to do what he said, but also to give myself some time to think about it all.

"While I was watching a film about Padre Pio one evening, something inside me broke, and I felt a strong need to confess. The next day, I called that man and told him I wanted to make my confession, as soon as possible. I was prepared to go anywhere to do it. I took a pen and paper and, for three days, prepared myself for that confession.

"A lot of things had piled up over the years, and my previous confessions had been superficial and without any repentance. I wanted it to be different this time, different from all the others. I prayed that the Holy Spirit would remind me of all the bad thoughts, words and deeds and omissions I had had. I prayed that after that confession I would feel like I had after my first confession. That man at church also gave me a prayer which, as I was preparing myself, I prayed so that priest would hear my confession as best he could. I could not sleep on the night before my confession. I could hardly wait for that moment.

"Finally I arrived at the confessional. I took out the papers from my bag, breathed deeply and said, 'I want to confess my sins that I have committed since the last valid confession, which was before my first communion.' 'OK,' the priest replied, 'You can begin to confess your sins.' The priest was amazed that I wanted to confess even the smallest sin, but I told him that I wanted to be completely clean and completely free, which he accepted gladly. He gave me his time and was truly like Jesus to me.

"The restlessness, the dissatisfaction and burden I had been carrying inside truly disappeared as I received absolution. They were silenced by a deep peace. The burden which I had been carrying until that moment was gone. Even the expression on my face changed.

"Two years have passed since then. I now go regularly to confession, once a month. My life changed after that confession, because I sincerely sought forgiveness for my sins. I did not seek any form of justification, nor did I try to diminish them. I wanted to be free. I repented deeply and sought forgiveness and, in return, I received much more, the peace I had lost and a new kind of life which is growing in me increasingly every day.

"After that confession, I began to be attracted by the presence of Jesus in the tabernacle. I would go to church and remain sitting for a long time after Mass, without praying anything. I was simply there, knowing that He was there too, spending time with Him and leaving the church with peace in my heart. The church I went to was the shrine of the Marija Bistrica. This lasted for about six months.

"Today I know that those months changed the course of my life completely. Things have already started happening to me which I couldn't have even dreamed about before. My favorite prayers are still simply spending time with Him without asking for anything. It seems that that is when He gives me the most.

"As a young woman, I am very sensitive to cleanliness of clothes, the house, and my whole environment. I like everything to be clean. So, I also like it when my soul is clean, and so I regularly have it cleaned through confession."

2. God as the Just and Loving Father

In our minds, we know that we became children of God, the Father, when we were baptised. But - in our times of need, do we turn to our heavenly Father gladly, and with confidence? Has anyone ever testified to us about his or her experience of God as the loving Father who truly cares for us? Do we really have confidence in Him?

Meeting with the Father in "heaven"*[1]

(*[1]Croatians use the same word for sky and heaven)

As for myself, it took me many years to meet God as the loving Father. It happened, a few years ago, on a flight to Ireland where I was conducting several evangelization meetings. I was reading John's Gospel and, suddenly, I realised there were a lot of sentences in which Jesus mentions His Father. I proceeded to count and highlight each 'Father' in this particular Gospel. Do you have any idea how many there are? I bet you have no better idea than I did. It appears more than one hundred times! Jesus describes God as His Father, who is also our Father, and then teaches us to pray with confidence to our Father.

Following this revelation, I begun to read with care. I took time to reflect on each sentence He utters about the Father, and begun to envision the love the Father has for us. The more time I spent reading Jesus' words about the Father, the more my heart opened to experience God as my loving Father.

After my eyes were opened, I discovered who the writers of the New Testament epistles prayed to – Jesus', and their, Father! I examined the words they prayed to Him. After some time, I also realized to whom most of the liturgical prayers are addressed – the Father! My time studying these prayers became a real blessing for me. My relationship with the Father changed drastically, and I know that He and I will work on perfecting it for the rest of my life.

To fill us with Father's love is one of the greatest jobs the Holy Spirit works within us (Romans 5:5). I can truly say that I, myself, for the first time in my life, met God as my loving Father in the heavens.

The Bible and the Church direct us to turn to the Father with confidence. Unfortunately I need to say this, without wanting to offend anyone: it is easy to tell by the way people say prayers to the Father, especially the "Our Father" (the

Lord's Prayer), whether they have a personal relationship with the Father, or whether they have only learned about Him as a concept.

Prayers are there, not just to be recited, but to be spoken with confidence, engaging our feelings in a very personal way. A prayer needs to come from the heart and not just from the mind. Anyone who hears it can easily tell the difference.

That does not mean that prayer has to be full of emotion, although it certainly may be. We cannot pretend before God, so it is normal for our personal prayers to be in line with our emotions. We cannot, for example, pray for our own child who has a difficult problem and exclude emotion from our prayers.

On the other hand, we can become overly emotional, but it does not necessarily demonstrate our faith. If we listen to ourselves pray, we will be able to discern whether our words reflect confidence, or the lack thereof. Our manner of speaking these words shows if we have an open door in our hearts to receive what we are asking for, or not.

How can we be in a mood to receive, if we do not understand what we are saying? Many Christians have prayed the Lord's Prayer their entire lives, but never actually understood it. Many Catholics also pray certain litanies, containing completely incomprehensible invocations, yet they have never felt the need to know what they are actually saying.

Sometimes we think we are demonstrating our faith just by saying prayers or performing rituals we do not understand. In point of fact, the opposite could be true.

Many believers say prayers they learned as children, but never understood, without making any effort to question them. Making an effort to understand what we truly are saying when we pray is more pleasing to God than just mindlessly reciting words. Understanding will change us, but our unwillingness to make any effort might mean that we do not really want to change ourselves.

Undoubtedly, there are truths which are hard to comprehend, but that is precisely where we need the help of the Holy Spirit. Only through His help can our knowledge constantly be perfected, and our prayers become increasingly comprehensible. Thus, praying the Lord's Prayer is something we perfect throughout our entire lives, by reflection, meditation and observation. Each new insight, even a very small one, can be seen as God's words directed to us, personally. This is particularly important in our relationship with our Heavenly Father.

If we think it sufficient to have a relationship with Jesus alone, then we do not believe that His words about the Father are meaningful in our own lives. How can we have confidence in Jesus if, at the same time, we do not have confidence in His words?

Isn't our lack of relationship with the Father one of the main hindrances to receiving God's mercy? If we relate to God the Father, through the image of any human being we call "father" (our own fathers or priests), then our image of the Heavenly Father can be more or less distorted.

This is why it is extremely important to accept God as our own Father. To have the Almighty God as our beloved and righteous Father gives our Christian life a completely new dimension.

If we want to know God as our Father, I suggest that you read carefully, and consider, each of the 103 times when Jesus, in John's Gospel, mentions His Father's name. Each of these references should become important to us as we reflect upon it. This may take some time, but I am sure that Jesus' words will draw us to God with confidence and intimacy, like a child drawing close enough to take his Father's hand.

A prophet said, a long time before Jesus' birth, that: "He will turn the hearts of sons to the Father" *. When we see Jesus we see the Father*. This investment of our time could change our entire future lives, on earth and in eternity. Be sure to read (remember, envision, reflect and pray) at least John's Gospel.

3. The Holy Spirit

Jesus says that He wants us to work together with the Holy Spirit, at all times. He said that He needed to go away so the Holy Spirit could come to us*.

Too many Christians today do not want Jesus to go, which is why they do not seek the relationship with the Holy Spirit that Jesus wants them to have. Jesus said that the Holy Spirit will guide us to "all truth" (John 16:12). Yet, we will not know all truth until eternity. Until then, we need the guidance of the Holy Spirit, every day of our lives.

After Jesus' ascension, we see that the apostles no longer communicate with Jesus, only with the Holy Spirit. They obeyed Jesus' words. In reading the Acts of the Apostles, pay attention to the apostles' relationship with the Holy Spirit.

How many Christians today have had the experience of cooperating with, much less communicating with, the Holy Spirit? What would our prayers and, indeed our very lives, be like if they were inspired by the Spirit? To work with the Holy Spirit means that we must communicate with Him. Jesus' sheep recognise His voice, and the Holy Spirit is the one who speaks Jesus' words to us (John 16:13-15). We need to communicate with the Spirit.

The Holy Spirit attracts believers because He is the love of the Father poured out into human hearts (Romans 5:5). That is why, for instance, crowds of people flock to Renewal in the Spirit meetings which encourage devotion to the Holy Spirit. They are able to sit for hours, patiently listening, praying and worshipping God, because they feel the love of God in the presence of the Holy Spirit.

When someone preaches under the inspiration of the Holy Spirit, the hearts of listeners burn like the hearts of the two disciples on the road to Emmaus*. The same thing happens in worship, praise and adoration. When the Holy Spirit manifests himself (appears or is revealed), no one looks at the clock; the limitations of time and space are no longer relevant.

Many believers have experienced prayer in which they lost all sense of time. Many say that when they pray, it is as though they enter another world, where they feel accepted and can find peace. Many Christians speak of moments of enlightenment while they pray, in which the Holy Spirit opens their minds to new understanding.

Those who have not experienced this, cannot understand it. If we can pass on to them our own experiences with the Holy Spirit, they might be attracted to think about it, envision it and, even, expect it.

The Holy Spirit and This Book

I prayed many times to the Holy Spirit while writing this book, truly wanting it to be a blessing to as many people, as possible. The Holy Spirit spoke to me on many occasions guiding me as I wrote. It is important to stress that, when we pray to the Holy Spirit about what we are doing, we need, first of all, to ask Him for His motivation, His purpose.

I, for example, needed His clear direction to write this book. Once I understood, I knew where my writing should go. It is the same with other tasks we undertake; we need to seek the direction, help and cooperation of the Holy Spirit.

When I write a chapter, most of the time it is either one extreme or the other: very hard going or flowing effortlessly. When my writing is difficult, I find it comes primarily from my human wisdom, without the help of the Spirit. When it is easy, then I know that the Holy Spirit is helping me. He gives me the ideas which I transform into words.

Of course, my finished product is never perfect. I must check what I have written, time and time again, to ensure the words are in agreement with the ideas I received by inspiration. If the reader pays attention, he will notice that some parts of the book read more easily than others. It all depends on how far I, as the writer, managed to follow the Holy Spirit's guidance.

We are blessed that the Holy Spirit is infinitely patient with us; He knows our human limitations. He is not disturbed when our work is imperfect. It is not difficult for Him to improve upon our efforts until both He, and we, are satisfied. If we have the right attitude, we will rejoice in whatever has been written by the Holy Spirit. He rejoices in the fact that, together, we have achieved something good which will be a blessing to others.

As soon as I received the English draft of this book, I gave it to an American friend who was visiting me and my family in Croatia. When she started reading it, she immediately discovered that many sentences were difficult to understand in English. I did not know that she had been an editor and proof reader during her career. The Holy Spirit knew! He sent her, at the right moment, thousands of miles from her home in California to finish His work. The result is the text you are reading now. The Holy Spirit likes to surprise us!

When we begin to share the Gospel: testifying about the work of the Holy Spirit and God's power in our lives, it will not immediately be easy. We may choose the wrong person, or the wrong time, or the wrong approach. However, if we have the right attitude, God will not consider our stumbling attempts as mistakes, but as our immaturity. He knows that the more trial and error, the sooner we will discover what works and what does not. Next time we will be wiser, more mature in God's ways.

The Holy Spirit wants us to realise that we are actually His pupils, or disciples, who will be learning throughout our entire lives. When we stop being pupils, we stop learning and moving towards perfection. We are called to be perfect, as our Father in Heaven is perfect. Anyone who sincerely believes, never loses his desire to be perfected.

4. The Kingdom of God

For a forty-day period following His resurrection, Jesus appeared to His disciples, teaching them about the Kingdom of God. From the Bible, we know that the Kingdom of God is in direct opposition to the Kingdom of Satan. Both kingdoms are well organised and constantly at war.

We know that there are good angels, evil spirits (fallen angels), saints, souls in purgatory, the Father, the Son, the Holy Spirit, and so forth, but do we know how it all works? What happens when we pray? To whom should we pray in specific circumstances, and how much prayer is necessary? What happens when we fast, when we worship, when we praise, when we seek?

At every Mass we encounter the entire Kingdom of God. Are we aware of that? Do we have any experiences related to the Kingdom of God?

Read the epistles, especially the Epistle to the Ephesians, to learn the basic facts about the two, very different, kingdoms. In this epistle, God asks us to become actively involved in the struggle of good against evil.

We should not think that everything that happens to us is according to God's will. We must resist the work of Satan; we should not accept his attacks as God's will towards us (Ephesians 6:10-20).

We did not receive the Holy Spirit to be able to accept our lives as they are, but to change them to be what the Lord wants them to be. If we have more experience with the Kingdom of God, our Christian lives will be more fruitful.

The Old Testament has much to say about the conflict between these two kingdoms. The Kingdom of God is frequently represented through God's chosen people – Israel. If Israel was in conflict with, or being attacked by, another nation, the priests and leaders would remind their soldiers of past victories, when their God had saved them. In that way priests and leaders trade with the talents Israel had (refer back to previous section on talents). These testimonies increased the soldiers' confidence in God. Inevitably, when they relied on their own strength, and not God's, they were defeated in battle.

In our own lives, we are often in conflict with superior enemies: serious illness, poverty, loneliness, feelings of rejection, guilt, inferiority, fear, problems with our children, etc. At times like these, we need the testimonies of people whom God has brought through similar circumstances.

We can find much inspiration in the biographies of the saints, especially contemporary saints like Padre Pio, Don Bosco, Mother Teresa, and so forth. If we have confidence in its help, the entire Church (the body of Christ on earth and in heaven) is with us. All who have ever been baptised into Christ and those who have died with Christ, are members of the Body of Christ – the Church.

On the Mount of Transfiguration, Jesus talked with Moses and Elijah to show us that we also can communicate with the saints in Heaven.

Those in Heaven respect our free will, as God Himself does, and can help us only if we ask (pray) with confidence. The same is true of the angels.

God will be as great in our lives as we allow Him to be, through our faith. We witness to each other when we need the help of the Kingdom of God. Here is a testimony from the Kingdom of God.

A New Heart – Through the Intercession of Pope John Paul II

Here is a testimony of healing through the intercession of saints – in this case, Pope John Paul II. The miracle is even more interesting, if we take into account that the healing is well documented by witnesses and medical reports:

"My name is Ante Z. I was born on 10 May 1993. I live in Retkovci, a small village in Croatia. From my childhood my parents taught me and talked about their faith. I finished elementary school and started going to high school. Gradually I got into a crowd which had no connection with faith or God. Every new day at school I got more and more deeply involved in this bad crowd. I was faced with various temptations, did a variety of stupid things, and sank deeper and deeper into sin. I began to swear, to have intense arguments with my parents and my sisters, to have physical fights with my schoolmates. Others began to be afraid of me, while I continuously looked for reasons to fight or argue.

"I already felt tired, dizzy and had pressure in my chest from time to time, but I didn't think it was important, and I continued to enjoy myself with my friends. When I spent time with them, I felt somehow strong and I thought no one could touch me. But slowly I began to have to pay the penalty for this kind of life: I failed the year at school, I began having problems with my parents, and I embarrassed my family. I just thought, 'Oh well, never mind, water under the bridge.' Nothing ever really 'touched' me.

My health problems became more frequent, so I decided to tell my parents. I started measuring my blood pressure and found that, along with all the other problems, it was very high. That scared me.

Dr. D.B. is a well-known cardiologist who also treats my father. After talking with my parents, I went to see Dr. D.B., thinking that he would give me some pills to normalise my blood pressure, and that would be that. When I came into his office, I panicked and had a 'bad feeling'. Another doctor, M.K., checked my heart with ultrasound, and I was watching his expression as he looked at the screen more intensely and, finally, with astonishment.

"There was a very long silence. It seemed to go on forever, or at least to me. I knew that something was wrong. After a few minutes, the doctor asked me if I got tired easily, if I was involved in any sports or hard physical work, which surprised me and, of course, I answered his questions positively.

"I went on looking at the screen showing a hole in my heart, but I thought that was normal, although I didn't understand anything. While all this was buzzing round my head, I heard him ask, 'Where's your father?' That frightened me more than anything. Then he called the first doctor, D.B., who came in with a woman doctor. They looked at the monitor for a long time, and just said, 'That's it.' After that we went back into the office where Dr. D.B. started to explain the findings to me. He told me, 'Well, we will have to operate on you; you have a hole in your heart 2.5 cm (1 in) in diameter.'

"Wow! What a shock! I couldn't believe it. My whole life flashed in front of me, and I said to myself, 'Jesus, it is all in your hands.' After they had repeated the examination, they confirmed the first result and explained that the procedure was almost routine these days, and that I would be able to lead a normal life. They would install some kind of 'umbrella' and everything would be fine. That made me feel a bit better. Then the doctor referred me to another hospital, to his colleague, who performs those operations, and his special skill was to 'fill up' holes in hearts.

From that moment, I turned to God, but thought, 'O God, why me?' My family started praying – my grandmother and eight of her friends started praying a novena. My father prayed to Blessed Pope John Paul II. Even before this situation, I had prayed to Pope John Paul II. I always had a great respect for our late Pope. His face, whenever I saw him on television, was somehow calm, and it gave me peace and strength to go on.

"The time came for me to go to hospital. I came into the hospital corridor with my parent. I asked about the doctor, and was told that he would be a bit late, so I should be patient. The corridor was full of people. While we were waiting for the doctor, I saw a man, who I would say was indigent, either an addict or a tramp. That man walked through the crowd and came up to me, offering his hand and said, 'So, you are Ante with the hole!' and I realised that this was the doctor who was going to perform my operation. I was totally shocked! I immediately realised that my God was involved in all this, which made me very happy. I went into the doctor's office. They had to record my heart through my throat. And then it began. Entering that room I said, 'Come on, Lord, you and I can do this.'

"All this time, my parents were waiting in the corridor and praying. The examination took a while, and the doctor looked in amazement at the computer screen, and muttered something to himself. I didn't understand anything he said, but I tried hard.

"When it was over, the doctor took all the test results I had brought and read them. I heard him saying, 'A hole, 2.5 cm (1 in) in diameter' and he went on muttering something else, but I didn't understand. He came up to me and said, 'Ante, you haven't got a hole! That is, I can see that there used to be one there, but it's healed and I can see the new part of your heart; it looks like there's a thin membrane stuck over that part.'

"Suddenly I was overcome with peace. I knew that God had healed me through the intercession of John Paul II. I came out, walked towards my parents and had the feeling that they already knew that there was no longer any hole, that I had been healed. When I told them, they went on looking at me calmly, and I laughed.

"Later, we all went to see Dr. S., and he told the same story – there was no hole, and that was that. But, just in case, and in view of the papers I had come with, he sent me to the hospital in Zagreb, so they could inject some dye into my veins to see where my blood was actually going. Of course, those results also showed that my blood was flowing normally. I said immediately, 'Thank you Lord, you have given me a new life!'

"From that day on, my life turned to my God, and my constant companion, Pope John Paul II, and I know that this healing happened because of his intercession. I realised how good God is and how much He means to me. Praise God! "

The testimonies, that people share with us, in person, can be even more compelling.

Pope John Paul 11

5. *The Church*

The experience of the Church, as the Body of Christ and as a community of believers, can be very different for different people. The experience depends on many factors:

How we feel about bishops, parish priests, religious instruction teachers, and our fellow believers;

How we feel about the pastoral work of our local community – the parish, the deaconry or diocese;

How we feel about the liturgy, the sacraments and liturgical prayer;

How we feel about the care provided for people in various needs, and especially the need for repentance and salvation.

We can experience the Church on a local level, from an awareness of our own parish, but also from a much broader point of view. We may have the opportunity to see how things work in other parishes, other dioceses and even other countries.

Personally, I see the Church from a worldwide prospective, because I have had the opportunity to visit many different dioceses and different countries. I have also had numerous opportunities to visit the Vatican, where I personally met the highest ranking representatives of the Church hierarchy.

I have met famous evangelists and many lay people with deep faith; they certainly witness what they believe by the way they live. I have had the opportunity to know people from other Christian denominations, to see how God is using them, and how they, in turn, view the Body of Christ as the Church. I have also had the opportunity to get to know the history of the Church.

It is to be expected that my experience of the Church will differ from the experience of those who have not had the chance to see it in a wider context.

My father taught me to study certain individuals and families, discerning/recognizing the connection between the way they lived out their faith and what ultimately happened to them. He taught me to observe everything around me in relationship to God. In this way, I learned what it means to be blessed, but also what it means to be cursed (Deutronomy 11:26).

I learned from the bad and good decisions I saw others make. I also learned to observe myself, my desire to be sinless, but how, as Saint Paul expressed it, I fall into sin in spite of all my efforts to resist*. In that way, I have learned to accept the weakness of others, because I realised that I, myself, am still weak.

We would expect that the Church would be the one community of believers who could live out their faith in an exemplary fashion. Yet, as we study those around us, we can distinguish the good from the bad, the mature from immature. As we observe closely the way certain people live their religion we discover many among "the first" who should be among "the last", and vice versa. There are people who never get noticed, who will one day "shine like stars in the heavens"*.

Let's Witness!

We should/must strive to live in accordance with the Gospel. Unbelievers will rarely gain true faith, if they do not recognise the supernatural God at work in believers. However well we behave, which we should do of course, it will not help us to evangelize, if the Holy Spirit and the power of God are not seen in the way we live. This is particularly important in multi-cultural environments, where people of various religions live together.

Good behaviour may draw people to the Church, but rarely will it draw them to God.

This is just as well, otherwise, people might be drawn to become Jehovah's Witnesses, Mormons or even Muslims, who often put Christians to shame. In some countries, they have more children, they dress more modestly, they abstain from alcohol (and some from tobacco), they attend religious services regularly and help one another much more willingly than many Christians do. And we are trying to convert them through our behaviour !

Our Christian lives should be testifying to what they do not have – the Holy Spirit and the mercy of a loving God; these sanctify and save us through the cross and resurrection of Jesus Christ.

Perhaps it would be valuable to begin new evangelism at seminaries and diocese meetings for priests. In that way, God's people would profit first and foremost, because no one has more opportunities to testify than parish priests. Laymen, actually experience God, by observing our own priests. They are the examples we should follow.

God Wants to Manifest Himself

Jesus and His followers revealed God to their generation in a marvelous way, but Jesus wants every generation, including today's, to witness demonstrations of His glory.

How do we know that Jesus really wants this for us too? Why do you think Jesus performed so many miracles in public? Anyone who has read the four Gospels carefully can find many instances when Jesus healed the sick and performed many other miracles in front of a large number of witnesses.

So, Jesus certainly wanted to show as many people as possible that He could, and would, perform miracles. Miracles and healings are not a private matter between God and man; they belong to the entire Church!

Jesus was revealing the Holy Spirit and the power of a loving God. Jesus simply had to perform supernatural deeds, and especially deeds of love, to reveal Himself as the Son of God. Otherwise, without these deeds to confirm His words, people would have had the right to call Him crazy, or a liar, or a fraud or a manipulator.

He did not claim to be merely a good man who loved people, nor a moral teacher, nor a religious leader, nor rabbi, nor a priest. He would not have needed miracles for that. He had to declare that He was the Son of God, but who would have believed Him, without the miracles? He, Himself, said that His deeds bore witness to Him.

In the end, the Jews condemned and killed Him because He claimed to be the Son of God. Their real motive, however, was envy. That is to say, the religious leaders were jealous because Jesus attracted larger crowds than they did; the people adored Him, not them.

If Jesus had proclaimed Himself to be the Son of God, without public miracles, He would have been killed early in His ministry. At the very least, He would have been scorned as a madman. Without the miracles (manifestations of the Holy Spirit and the power of God, prophesied about the Messiah)*, very few would have believed He was speaking the truth.

Jesus left us a mandate to testify to other people. He, Himself, said that His works testified that He was God. The risen Jesus lives in every generation and His words are proclaimed to every generation. Jesus has been performing signs and wonders down through the ages. Why not now?

Many saints were contemporaries of our grandparents: Padre Pio, Don Bosco and others. God marked (honored, distinguished) their lives with an incredible number of miraculous manifestations.

In the case of Padre Pio alone, the Church has acknowledged at least one hundred miracles, though he performed many more. God has preserved his body completely incorruptible, although he died years ago in 1968.

The Church has ascribed more miracles to Padre Pio that to Lourdes or Fatima, but still very little is said about him from the pulpit or in religious education classes. In point of fact, nothing is taught about him at Catholic schools. As far as I know, not a single church in Croatia has been dedicated in his name.

Are we not at fault in cases like this? Here God has revealed Himself powerfully and conspicuously in those like Padre Pio who is a sign of Jesus' resurrection through his miraculous life. Yet we, as believers, do not use enough our God-given opportunities to witness to others. People are seeking God, but how are they going to hear about Him without our testimonies?

Saint Pio of Pietrelcina 1887 - 1968

God is Manifest in Miracles

In every generation, and in the life of every believer, God wants to be manifest as the almighty God who loves men and, through His great love and mercy, He performs miracles. Every believer is called to be a participant in God's miracles.

How do we define a miracle? A miracle is anything that could never happen without God's intervention.

This includes not just healing and deliverance, but also repentance, conversion, love and forgiveness for our enemies, true compassion for the needy, deliverance from fear, anger, rejection, guilt, inferiority and peace in difficult situations. One of the greatest miracles is the forgiveness we receive from God and the forgiveness we, therefore, are able to extend to our enemies. Many Christians have had incredible experiences of forgiveness.

When we are bearing the burden of a serious sin in our souls, it can create deep feelings of guilt, inferiority, rejection and many other things that deprive us of peace. The instant we can accept God's forgiveness, all that disappears. Many people can testify that, at the moment they received absolution for their sins, they met God as immeasurable unconditional love for the first time. They experienced that peace which the world does not know and only God can give*.

God seeks every opportunity to answer our prayers, so that we can testify to His resurrection. He is the living, risen, almighty God, whose other name is Love. Who will believe us if He does not confirm His Love by works? We must allow Jesus to be alive in our lives; unbelievers need to see Him as the risen and living God in us.

What Will He Do?

Jesus longed for people to seek to know Him, to gain confidence in Him and receive God's love and grace by preparing their hearts for His coming. How did He do this? He used to send His disciples ahead to proclaim His coming to the towns and villages. He even gave them authority to heal and deliver people*.

When the disciples came into a town, they would testify about what Jesus had said and done. Then they would perform healings and deliverances among the local people. Listening to the testimony of the disciples and seeing what these "simple" men could do*, people had to wonder how much more their teacher, Jesus, would do. By the time Jesus arrived, their hearts were full of expectation and confidence.

Suppose we put ourselves in their shoes! Would our faith in Jesus be the same without any previous proclamation – the testimony of His disciples? Of course, we would expect their teacher to do what His disciples could not do. Jesus' disciples have the same task today: to proclaim the Christ (the Messiah) who is to come.

Let us seek within ourselves, the courage to proclaim Christ. Let us find in our own lives, the treasure we have as those redeemed by Christ, and as His disciples. Let us testify about who God is to us personally, what He has done for us and how!

We have to know that "God is still in the miracle-working business". These miracles show us the living God. Once we have personally experienced His grace and mercy, we can begin to experience Him in various other ways, in prayer, in the liturgy, in the sacraments, in our families and our everyday lives. We have been created as unique individuals who have varying amounts of faith. The experience of His grace should lead us to embrace/seek God as a person. If His mercy is so overwhelming, how much greater is He, in person!

Jesus said that those who have not seen, but still believe, are blessed. The apostles did not believe in His resurrection, even though several women testified that they had seen Him alive*. Jesus rebuked them. Thomas had to place his finger in Jesus' wounds to be able to believe*. In His great mercy, Jesus allowed him to do that. In the same way, He allows us to be convinced.

We, personally, may not need miracles to believe in Jesus' resurrection and in His real presence in the Eucharist. Let us not judge those who, like the apostles, do need God's grace to be able to believe. Let us do all we can to help them believe!

Conclusion

Evangalism is not the ministry of a chosen few. Every believer is called to evangelize, to share the Gospel, to testify to his own faith. Each of us has received at least one talent, even though we may not be aware of it yet. It may not be evident in our lives and, consequently, we do not appreciate its value.

Some people have felt God's closeness and been blessed by His goodness many times, but that does not mean that every experience has become a talent. We should not expect all our experiences to be talents.

Any experience can be brief or long-term, full of passion or totally emotionless. Sometimes we need to pray and ponder, at length, before we can unearth our talents. Personally, I have experienced many blessings from God, but my most valuable talent has been the exemplary faith of my parents.

I was brought up in a traditional Catholic family with five brothers and two sisters. We did not miss a single Mass, and prayed together frequently during the day. Witnessing the faith of my parents, and observing their confidence in God's provision for our daily needs, caused me to accept God as the most important thing in my life.

My grandmother, a widow for many years, was a godly woman of prayer. Through her testimony, she brought me closer to the Holy Spirit and the Blessed Virgin Mary. Her belief furthered my own confidence in God.

After I grew up, a priest testified to me about the work of the Holy Spirit in his life. His testimony was very attractive to me, increasing my resolve to trust God, and especially His Word, even more. Since that time, as I am reading the Bible, I find myself relating to the testimonies of many Bible characters. This constantly stimulates, encourages and changes me, maturing my relationship with God.

During the more than twenty years I have been active as an evangelist, I have met many people whose experiences have touched my heart, drawing me ever closer to God. Through all these experiences I have become a more mature believer and a better person - I have been constantly evangelized.

We must search out our talents to be able to trade with them, and also to praise God for them. Our thankfulness increases the worth of our talents. A talent becomes then, a pearl of great price*, given only to those who are ready to receive it.

Jesus encourages us with His words, "If anyone is thirsty, let him come to me and drink!" (John 7:37). We should not waste our talent on those who are not "thirsty" to receive it. We don't want it to be trampled underfoot by swine (Matthew 7:6). We must look for patiently for the opportune moment when a thirsty person appears.

The Gospel of Jesus Christ, offering His salvation and redemption, is not some kind of shoddy doctrine to be peddled to others by any means possible. We should always remember, as we share the good news (the Gospel), that Jesus paid in full for our forgiveness (redemption), with His innocent blood. We must be witnesses. Those with whom we share the Gospel need to see how much we appreciate our own salvation and redemption. They can deduce that from the way we witness.

There are many excellent teachers and plenty of spiritual literature in the Church today. On the other hand, there are too few witnesses, willing to offer "water to the thirsty" at the opportune moment.

This book has been a labor of love for me, not only love for all believers and non-believers, but also my love, thanks and praise to my Triune God: the Father, the Son, and the Holy Spirit. I pray that you, the reader, will open your heart, not only to receive the God's grace, but also to pass it on.

" May the Lord bless you and keep you.

May the Lord make his face to shine upon you,

and be gracious to you.

May the Lord lift up his countenance upon you,

and give you His Peace."

"Do not be afraid.

Do not be satisfied with mediocrity.

Put out into the deep and let down your nets for a catch."

Pope John Paul 11

The Rosary - *prayer of my spirit*

Is praying the rosary a joy for you?
Do you really feel that your prayers are being granted through the rosary?
Does it ever happen to you, that while praying the rosary, various names of people suddenly come to you?
Did you ever have an interior vision at the time of the rosary?
Did you ever have a strong emotional or physical experience during the rosary?
Do you feel as if you are 'outside time' during the rosary?
This best selling book will answer these questions for you, as well as helping you to fall in love with this devotion.

Power from on High

The power from on high (the power of the Holy Spirit) which we receive at the sacrament of confirmation, and which is so powerful that it can change the human heart, acts in completely unexpected ways: through dreams, visions and prophecies. There is almost no one who doesn't dream, many people have visions, but also we often have the impression that God is speaking to us through other people. The Bible is full of dreams, visions and prophecies...
This is a book which brings together forever the power of the Holy Spirit with dreams, prophecies and visions!

Books by Josip Loncar translated from Croatian

into the English language are published by :

JESMAR PRESS

Email: jesmarpress@gmail.com   Website: www.jesmarpress.com